THE SMART PROBLEM SOLVER

PRATEEK VASISHT

Copyright © 2024 Prateek Vasisht

All rights reserved

No part of this book may be reproduced, or stored in a retrieval system, or transmitted in any form or by any means, electronic, mechanical, photocopying, recording, or otherwise, without express written permission of the publisher.

ISBN: 9798339799603

CONTENTS

Introduction 1

Problem solving 5

The Problem-Solver's Map 15

The Problem-Solver's Model 23

    Discover the Problem 31

    Define the Goal 53

    Devise the Solution 63

    Deploy the Solution 81

The Problem-Solver's Mindset 91

Afterword 101

References 105

Appendices 107

    1. Problem Solving Questions 108

    2. Problem Solving Worksheet 110

    3. Problem Solving Canvas 112

    4. Case Study 114

About the Author 123

THE SMART PROBLEM SOLVER

INTRODUCTION

Problems! They come in all shapes and sizes. We face them all the time and in all contexts. It could be designing a new product for an organization, fixing a faulty machine, deciding to move house or even solving a sudoku puzzle. While they may seem different, they all share one underlying characteristic. It is always about a gap - relative to some thing or some condition. The goal is to close the gap. The challenge is to find the best solution for doing so. The common structure of problems becomes the very tool with which we can accomplish this challenge. The purpose of this book is to bring to light the fundamental process for solving problems that can be applied to all types of situations.

While the methodology presented can be applied to personal and professional situations, the book is written with everyday problem solving in mind. It is written to help people solve problems they face in their daily lives, using an approach that is intuitive, natural and cognitively light. It is written to provide a framework that can be used by anyone, anywhere, to structure and solve any problem.

Given the broad scope, the book uses an intuitive QUESTION-BASED approach to maximize application across contexts and audiences. Problem-solving is essentially a sequence of inquiries and analysis. The intention is to distil the essence of problem solving into a series of interrogations that can be used to understand, structure and solve any problem. By doing this, I hope to present problem-solving in its most fundamental sense, and in a manner that is natural, practical and widely applicable.

Problem solving is a core life skill. We use it in every aspect of our personal lives. It is also highly valued in the workplace, consistently ranking as one of the most sought-after skills by employers. By applying a robust and reliable approach, we can tackle problems with greater confidence, and with greater expectation of success. Proficient problem-solvers are well-placed to assist not only themselves but also those around them, and are frequently regarded as leaders.

Problem solving is a capability. Like everything else, practice makes perfect. The practice however should be the right type of practice. This book provides a systematic and practical thought process to help improve problem-solving capabilities.

To set the theme, the first chapter establishes the benefit of using a structured approach for problem solving, and introduces the MAP-MODEL-MINDSET METHODOLOGY - on which the book is based. Problem solving, as an analytical exercise, can be viewed as a journey and a process. The methodology incorporates both facets. The MAP presents problem solving via the metaphor of a journey. The MODEL presents the fundamental process that can be used to solve any problem. The third aspect, MINDSET, outlines the crucial mental approaches that amplify the effectiveness of our thinking and decision-making. Successful problem solving requires the appropriate toolset, skill-set and mindset. Map-Model-Mindset is a holistic problem-solving methodology that contains all these aspects. It provides the complete blueprint for better and smarter problem solving.

With the framework set, the remaining chapters elaborate the Map, Model and Mindset. First up, the four questions that make up the Map are presented: *Where are we now? Where do we want to be? How can we get there? How to ensure we are there?* Following that, the Model is introduced, with a chapter dedicated to each of the four steps of the problem-solving process (Discover-Define-Devise-Deploy). For each step, the characteristic questions are covered and a heuristic method is presented. The final chapter discusses the three mindsets (Critical Thinking, Balance, Dynamism).

Aligned with the book's practical focus, the information presented in the book is condensed into a set of resources for readers to apply in future problem-solving endeavours. To illustrate the problem-solving approach, two case studies are included. The first covers a typical problem encountered in organizational settings. The second covers a classic personal conundrum. For the reader's benefit, selected quotes that help sharpen our thought processes are also interspersed throughout the book.

The methodology and questions presented in this book provides an intuitive and comprehensive framework for the reader to develop into a SMART PROBLEM SOLVER. It is my sincere wish that you will find enjoyment and value in the pages of this book.

All the best!

PROBLEM SOLVING
Chapter 1: Map-Model-Mindset

Problem solving is an innate activity that we undertake throughout our lives in various capacities. At home we could be wondering about what to do about a faulty washing machine, how to arrange a meeting with friends who have conflicting availabilities or whether to replace an ageing car. It is also a part of our workplace activities, be it diagnosing something (or someone), responding to a scenario or designing a new product to solve an unmet need. While the context or challenge may differ, all these activities have problem solving at their core.

What is problem solving? To understand, we need to look at the key term – problem. Generally speaking, a problem is a situation that needs to be addressed. It arises due to a discrepancy between the current state and a target state. It may involve restoring something (or someone) to normal condition. Equally, it may involve achieving an open-ended aspiration. Either way, there is a gap with respect to something, some state, some condition or some ambition. This gap is usually peculiar and hence requires considered effort to resolve. Take the example of a room in a house. It is evening and the room is dark (current state). We want to illuminate the room (target state). To do so, we switch on the lights. This is a normal course of events. There is only one obvious solution and it is straightforward to the point of being an automatic action. There is no challenge. No peculiar gap. This cannot be classified as a true problem. Now consider if we switched on the lights to find the bulb was fused. The situation is now out of the ordinary. This is a problem. It is a very simple one, but still requires the effort of replacing the fused bulb with a working one. Discrepancy and effort. These two attributes are inherent to every true problem. We have a gap, discrepancy or issue - and we need to do something about it. A problem is precisely this predicament, captured in question format: what to do about [a situation]?

A PROBLEM IS A QUESTION OR SITUATION THAT NEEDS TO BE RESOLVED. PROBLEM SOLVING IS THEN THE PROCESS OF DEVISING AND DEPLOYING A SOLUTION TO ADDRESS THE PROBLEM.

STRUCTURED PROBLEM SOLVING

Our approach to solving problems can range from slapdash to meticulous. Unstructured thinking is fast and uncontrolled. Structured thinking is slower but controlled. Structured thinking involves undertaking a systematic process to study (and solve) a problem. By being systematic, we can seek and analyse a broader number of inputs. This allows us to build a truer and better picture of the problem at hand. It also prevents us from jumping to conclusions. As a result, we have greater confidence in solutions resulting from systematic analyses. Systematic approaches, by their very nature, are traceable and repeatable. By being systematic, we create a logical audit trail that can be useful if we want to review a decision, strategy or outcome at a later point. We can also re-apply a structured approach to other problems, something that, by definition, cannot be done at all for unstructured approaches or done very weakly for semi-structured approaches. By being systematic we are also better placed to control for various cognitive biases. Structured thinking adds rigour to the problem-solving process. This vastly improves our ability to devise suitable and successful solutions.

IDEALLY, A STRUCTURED APPROACH SHOULD BE USED FOR ALL PROBLEM SOLVING. Two barriers however impede this ideal from being achieved. The first barrier is perceived cognitive load. Sometimes, a problem may not seem big enough to justify the time and effort of applying a structured approach. Other times, we may simply not have the inclination to adopt a systematic process, thereby falling into the seductive trap of unstructured approaches whose apparent "efficiency" comes at the cost of rigour. The second barrier is knowledge. A structured problem-solving model may not readily come to mind, may not seem to apply, or indeed, may not even be known. This is applicable particularly to everyday situations. In our professional lives, we might have access to models and processes for structured thinking. In our everyday lives however, this is often not the case. Yet, the problems we face in our personal lives are just as important or complex. As a result of these two barriers, we often end up adopting approaches that sacrifice either rigour or application (or both!).

To achieve the ideal of using a structured approach for all problem solving, we need an approach that is detailed enough to be meaningful yet broad enough to apply to the widest type of problems. We need an approach with the right composition: one that is intuitive, robust, and has a manageable cognitive load. All problems have the same underlying mechanics. These underlying common properties can be used to develop a structured approach that is common to all problem solving. By adopting an approach that has the right level of structure, and is focussed on fundamentals, we can equip ourselves to handle problems of any type, efficiently and effectively.

The premise of this book is that structured problem solving can, and should be applied to all situations. The purpose of this book is to present an intuitive methodology for structured problem solving, that can be used to solve problems of all types, in all contexts.

> *"EACH PROBLEM THAT I SOLVED BECAME A RULE WHICH SERVED AFTERWARDS TO SOLVE OTHER PROBLEMS"* – RENE DESCARTES

THE MAP-MODEL-MINDSET METHODOLOGY

Problem solving can be conceptualized as a journey and a process. As a journey, it is about navigating from problem to solution. As a process, it is about accomplishing the journey in a systematic and robust manner. When solving problems, we need to shift between these points of view. To successfully resolve problems, we need the best mental vantage point. To do this, we need to zoom in and out of the details of a problem, as required. In addition to this ability to shift perspective, effective problem solving also correlates with certain types of analytical dispositions or mindsets. Successful problem solving is therefore about three things: journey, process and capability. It is about understanding what we are doing, doing it systematically and maximizing results for a given level of input. There is problem solving and then there is *smart* problem solving. To accomplish the latter, we need a methodology that caters to all three dimensions. With this in mind, the MAP-MODEL-MINDSET METHODOLOGY has been developed. It visualizes problem solving as a holistic framework with three components: Map (journey), Model (process), and Mindset (capability).

The Map provides a means to plot our overall problem-solving journey. The Model, which corresponds to the Map, is the systematic process that we use to solve the problem. Supporting the Model, and by extension the entire problem-solving endeavour, are some proven mindsets that help us solve problems with greater potency.

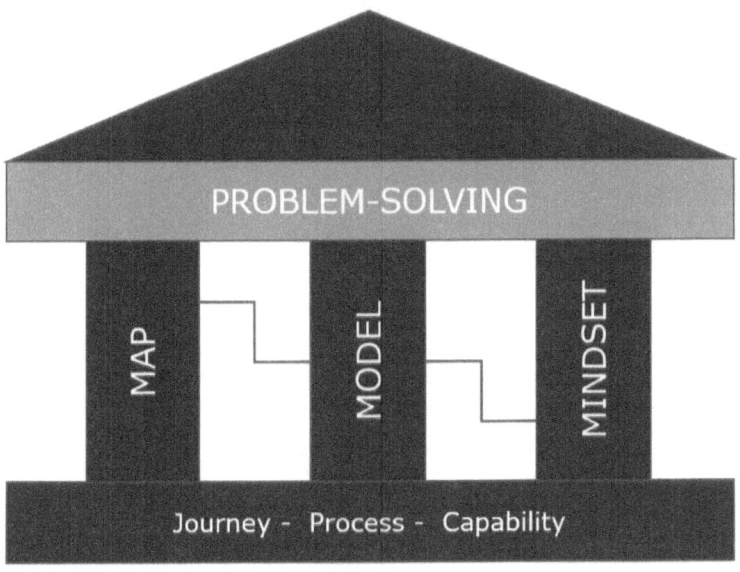

Figure 1: Map Model Mindset methodology

The Model, which represents the fundamental problem-solving process, lies at the heart of the methodology. This is the component that we use to actually solve problems. The Map and Mindset are accompaniments to the Model. The Map is a conceptual abstraction of the Model. It is useful for framing and visualizing our overall approach. Mindset is the power source, that enables us to follow the problem-solving process described in the Model with maximum effect.

Using a driving analogy, the Map is, well, the map, the Model is the actual driving and the Mindset is the skill of the driver. The Map is the concept; Model, the practical execution; Mindset, the proficiency. When all three align, we can visualize the big picture, execute detail, and do so very potently.

INTUITIVE APPROACH

Problem solving is essentially a sequence of inquiries and analyses. Asking questions comes naturally to us. By asking the right questions in the right sequence, we can engage with a problem in an intuitive manner, while maintaining a healthy level of rigour. With this in mind, this book adopts a natural-language QUESTION-BASED APPROACH.

We make sense of our world by asking questions. It's an innate response and the first step in gathering information and building knowledge. An approximate analogy would be traveling to a country where a different language is spoken. If you're fluent in the language, that's great. If not, you must rely on more universal and intuitive methods of communication, such as facial expressions and hand gestures. By using questions to structure and solve problems, we harness a natural tendency to acquire a fundamental, intuitive and universal method, that can be used to solve any problem.

The Map (journey) and Model (process) components of the methodology are described in terms of their characteristic questions. These questions, when asked and answered in the sequence presented, allow us to progress from problem to solution in a robust and comprehensive manner.

Map-Model-Mindset is a holistic methodology that can help structure any problem-solving endeavour. Its components are detailed in the following chapters.

> *"GIVE ME A PLACE TO STAND AND A LEVER LONG ENOUGH AND I WILL MOVE THE WORLD"* –
> *ARCHIMEDES*

Σ

"TO ASK THE RIGHT QUESTION IS ALREADY HALF THE SOLUTION TO A PROBLEM" – CARL JUNG

THE PROBLEM-SOLVER'S MAP

Chapter 2: Visualizing the journey

A map is a representation. It represents the real world around us, making it both a tool for orientation and navigation. Problem solving is also a journey and, by virtue of that, requires both orientation and navigation. The Map is thus the first part of our trilogy for solving problems. It provides a generic approach that can be used to solve problems of any type.

> *"HE WHO LOVES PRACTICE WITHOUT THEORY IS LIKE THE SAILOR WHO BOARDS SHIP WITHOUT A RUDDER AND COMPASS AND NEVER KNOWS WHERE HE MAY CAST"* – LEONARDO DA VINCI

COMPONENTS OF THE MAP

The Map contains four components which represent the problem-solving journey. The journey commences by understanding the current state and concludes by having a confirmation that we have reached the desired state. The components are presented as four questions. These are questions that we naturally ask during the course of solving a problem, either deliberately or sub-consciously. By codifying them as components, the Map supports our ideal of adopting a systematic question-based approach. As shown later, the questions of the Map will integrate naturally with the questions presented in the Model.

WHERE ARE WE NOW?

The very first step in the problem-solving journey is orientation: getting the bearings on where we are standing now with respect to the problem. What is the current state of affairs? What is the current meter reading? What is the scenario? What is the current reality? This is an honest description of what we are seeing, feeling and observing now. Using the metaphor of a journey, this is the "starting point", as interpreted for the prevailing context.

WHERE DO WE WANT TO BE?
The next step is visualizing the desired future. What is the end result we want? What is the condition, behaviour or target we want to accomplish? This is the achievement that will solve the problem. Using the metaphor of a journey, this is the "destination", as interpreted for the prevailing context.

HOW CAN WE GET THERE?
Knowing our destination, we can now chart out the best way for reaching it. This question represents the chosen strategy or choice for reaching our destination. Using the metaphor of a journey, this is the "route", as interpreted for the prevailing context.

HOW TO ENSURE WE ARE THERE?
The last component includes two actions. The first is taking action. Using the journey metaphor, this is putting the foot on the pedal and driving on the route. It is also about verifying that we have indeed reached our destination via some observation. In a journey, this would be a sign or landmark. In problem-solving, it will be an action plan and some indicator(s) to verify the achievement of the goal.

Figure 2: The Journey

THE *WHY* FACTOR

The Map is a high-level planning and assessment tool. To get more out of the Map, we can add another component to it. It is an interrogative adverb, and a very powerful one: *Why*. By asking *Why* for each of the four components, we can conduct a much deeper diagnosis. We have seen the four questions of the Map. Now, we add a *Why* to each question:

- WHERE ARE WE NOW?
    - Why are we here?
    - [Why did the problem happen?]
- WHERE DO WE WANT TO BE?
    - Why do we want to be there?
    - [Why will this be our goal?]
- HOW CAN WE GET THERE?
    - Why will we get there this way?
    - [Why will we use this solution strategy?]
- HOW TO ENSURE WE ARE THERE?
    - Why did we want to be here?
    - [Why did we want this result?]

Adding one question dramatically enhances the insights we can gain. Adding *Why* to the first two questions facilitates a deeper analysis of the rationale behind the problem and the goal. Adding *Why* to the last two questions facilitates a deeper analysis of the rationale behind our strategy and the outcomes we wish to realize. The WHY FACTOR, as it can be called, turbo-charges every analysis we conduct. By surfacing underlying causes and motivations, asking *Why* helps us build a rationale-chain. It allows us to validate our conclusions and decisions at every step of the problem-solving journey, and solve problems with clarity, coherence, and confidence.

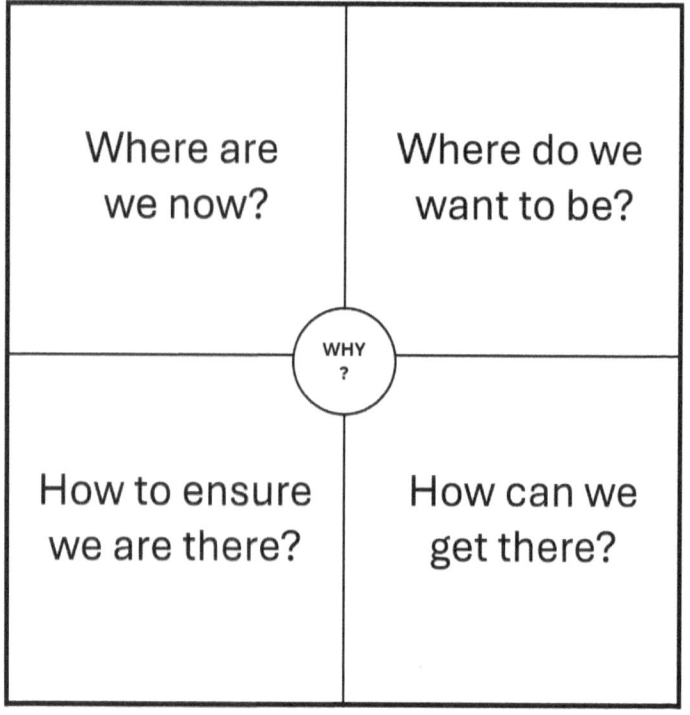

Figure 3: The Map

"THE NOBLEST PLEASURE IS THE JOY OF UNDERSTANDING" – LEONARDO DA VINCI

USING THE MAP

Often, when faced with a problem, our instinct is to attempt to solve it mentally. For simple problems, that can work. For more involved problems, it does not work very well. We tend to over-estimate how many things we can hold and process mentally. For complex problems, the act of writing down the problem significantly enhances our ability to solve it. Transcribing a thought onto paper requires a level of mental processing. What we write down is already one step more refined than our initial thought. Things that are written down can also be visualized better.

THE MAP IS A HIGH-LEVEL TOOL THAT WE CAN USE TO PLAN, PREVIEW AND REVIEW OUR PROBLEM-SOLVING EFFORT. Its best use is right at the beginning: to solve the problem at a conceptual and abstract level before delving into details. Using the Map puts us in a frame of mind to simulate the generic problem-solving journey that is common to problems of all types.

While the best use for the Map is at the beginning, it can actually be used at any step of the problem-solving endeavour to see the proverbial "forest from the trees". When we are deep into problem solving, the Map allows us to zoom-out and review the big picture, and our rationale, free from the mazy distraction of details. The questions of the Map can be used to explain a problematic situation, and the broad resolution strategy, in a manner that is easy to understand. It also serves as an excellent aide for visual presentation. In situations where other stakeholders are involved, and in particular if their approval is required, being able to offer a high-level precis of the problem and solution by using natural-language questions is highly beneficial.

The components (questions) of the Map correspond directly with the four steps of problem-solving Model, which is discussed next.

Σ

"ALL YOU NEED IS THE PLAN, THE ROAD MAP, AND THE COURAGE TO PRESS ON TO YOUR DESTINATION" – EARL NIGHTINGALE

THE PROBLEM-SOLVER'S MODEL

Chapter 3: Visualizing the process

Laying at the heart of the MAP – MODEL - MINDSET methodology, the Model delves into the details of problem solving. It provides a systematic process that can be used to solve problems of any type.

The Model comprises four steps that logically stem from, and directly correlate with, the four quadrants of the Map.

> *"MOST PEOPLE SPEND MORE TIME AND ENERGY GOING AROUND PROBLEMS THAN IN TRYING TO SOLVE THEM" – HENRY FORD*

COMPONENTS OF THE MODEL

The Map depicts the problem-solving journey. The Model provides the corresponding process to accomplish this journey. A process is a mechanism to transform inputs into outputs. The problem-solving process takes in an input (problem) and transforms it into an output (solution).

All problems share a common structure. They centre around a discrepancy caused by a peculiar situation that requires some effort to resolve. Problem solving is then the process of traversing that gap. Problems therefore are always about a starting point (current state), an end-point (goal), and, a strategy to bridge the gap (solution). Following from this, there is a fundamental approach that can be used to solve problems of all types. The Model presents this process in a distilled and authentic format.

Problem-solving is a four-step process (Discover – Define – Devise – Deploy). The first two steps ensure that we are solving the *right* problem. The next two steps relate to solving the problem *right*.

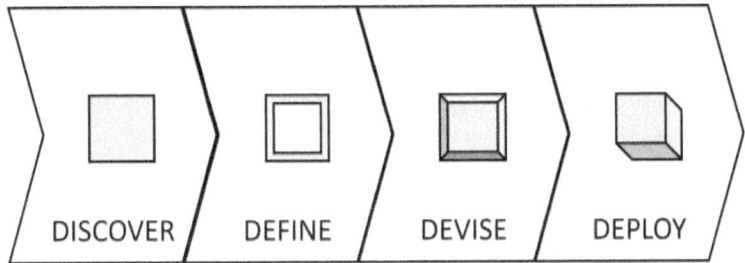

Figure 4: The Model

The steps of the Model, and their relation to the Map questions is shown below. A graphical representation of this, is found in the Problem-Solving Canvas, provided in the Appendix 3.

- DISCOVER THE PROBLEM:
    - what is the problem really about?
    - "WHERE ARE WE NOW?
- DEFINE THE GOAL:
    - what would success look like?
    - WHERE DO WE WANT TO BE?
- DEVISE THE SOLUTION:
    - how could we solve the problem?
    - HOW CAN WE GET THERE?
- DEPLOY THE SOLUTION:
    - what is our action plan?
    - HOW TO ENSURE WE'RE THERE?

> *"IF YOU CAN'T DESCRIBE WHAT YOU ARE DOING AS A PROCESS, YOU DON'T KNOW WHAT YOU'RE DOING"* – WILLIAM EDWARDS DEMING

USING THE MODEL

Problem solving is an analytical exercise. Our first encounter with a problem is typically by noticing a symptom or indicator. We may not know all the details. The path to the solution may also be unclear. A problem is a challenge. The Model is a tool to combat this challenge.

To solve a problem, we undertake a process. While there can be many representations of this process, with varying level of detail and specificity, at its core, problem solving is about four steps: understanding the problem, identifying the goal, devising a solution, and implementing it. Starting with problem discovery, we progress sequentially across the steps. The steps are inter-related: the outputs of one become inputs into the other. By being discrete yet inter-related, each step brings its own unique importance in the process. Doing one step well sets us up nicely for doing the next step well.

For simpler problems, there are only a handful of parameters to work through. The possible solutions or exemplars have generally been pre-established. As problems become more complex, the parameters increase and the solutions become increasingly undefined. For simple problems, we can work through the Model in more-or-less a linear fashion. Complex problems will likely involve revision, rethinking and iteration. This is part of the process. While the Model is depicted linearly, it is in practice dynamic and iterative. Iteration however must not be conflated with structure. The steps of the Model are fundamental to problem solving of all kinds. Iteration is a practical matter of course.

The upcoming chapters describe the four steps of the Model. Problem solving is about asking the right questions, in the right sequence. In line with our question-based approach, each step is described in terms of key interrogations that characterize it. For each process step, a Method is also identified. This serves as a mental shortcut, heuristic or tool to help answer the questions pertaining to each step.

The Problem-Solving Worksheet (Appendix 2) contains a summary of the questions and methods for each step of the Problem-Solving Model.

Σ

"SUCCESS IS A SCIENCE; IF YOU HAVE THE CONDITIONS, YOU GET THE RESULT" – OSCAR WILDE

PUT INTO PRACTICE

Aligned with the book's practical approach, two fictional case studies are used to illustrate the questions and methods that will be explored in the forthcoming four chapters.

HOLLAND CHOCOLATES

Holland Chocolates is experiencing a consistent decline in profits, and seeks strategies for recovery.

It is a good exemplar for problems where there is a variance (gap) from an established target that needs to be bridged. It represents a typical theme for problems encountered in work settings. This case study will be worked through in Chapters 4-7. Fun fact: the original inspiration for the methodology presented in this book traces back to solving a similar problem!

CAREER CRISIS

Hans, a middle-aged executive, is grappling with diminishing career opportunities and seeks a way out from this conundrum.

It is a good exemplar for problems where there is a gap between the current state and an open-ended, or undefined, desired future state, which is often the case with (fuzzy) personal problems. Many people go through a career or mid-life crisis and it can be very bewildering; further justifying its selection as a case study. It is presented in Appendix 4.

Remember, all problems have the same fundamental characteristics. The Map and Model, which are combined in the PROBLEM-SOLVING CANVAS can be used to solve any problem, be it: dealing with a faulty dishwasher, reviewing an investment portfolio, moving house, weeding a garden, or even transforming an organization!

DISCOVER THE PROBLEM
Chapter 4: What is happening?

The *Discover* step corresponds to the Map question: *Where are we now*? It is about finding out what is happening. Its purpose is to describe the current situation in a concise and objective manner. Research and analysis lie at the heart of this step. The quality of the insights gained in this step correlate directly with how well we frame the problem, and therefore, how well we solve it.

Discovery is foundation of problem solving. Being the first step, we start with a symptom or indicator. The task on hand is to substantiate this observation with research and analysis. To fully understand the problem, we need to employ a broad scope of inquiry: ranging from high level overview to granular detail, and encompassing both quantitative and qualitative data. While the depth of the inquiry will depend on the problem, it will typically centre around a set of interrogations. There are 7 questions in total. These correspond to the sequence of activities that lie at the heart of discovery: OBSERVATION, EXPLORATION AND DISTILLATION. The first question is about the initial observation. The next 5 relate to broadening the enquiry to fully explore the problem. The last question is about distilling the critical factors, levers or causes.

> *"DISCOVERY IS SEEING WHAT EVERYBODY ELSE HAS SEEN, AND THINKING WHAT NOBODY ELSE HAS THOUGHT" – ALBERT SZENT-GYORGYI*

WHAT HAS COME TO OUR ATTENTION?

This step is about the indicators or symptoms that capture our attention initially. It could be an event, a realization, a trend, or any gap from a desired or target state. It could have happened in the past, be happening now, or even be a forecast.

A symptom is the starting point for a diagnosis. The nature of the problem then determines the level of analysis required. For simple problems, the linkages between cause and effect are known or easily inferred. We can progress quickly from symptom to diagnosis on the basis of an established procedure or model. For complex problems these linkages must be determined by research and analysis.

An indicator is an early sign of a problem. The apparent problem is not always the real problem. It is therefore prudent to consider it as such - an element that has surfaced at first glance. Take, for instance, a washing machine drum that doesn't drain post-wash (symptom). The fundamental cause could be related to the wash cycle, the drainage pipe, or another factor. While the initial symptom may not be the underlying cause, it will require resolution. For the washing machine, the solution, in every case, will entail ensuring the drum empties after a wash cycle.

The first step in problem-solving should be to demarcate separately the indicator or symptom, recognizing it as possibly both a part of, and separate from, the actual problem to be addressed.

"DON'T BECOME A MERE RECORDER OF FACTS, BUT TRY TO PENETRATE THE MYSTERY OF THEIR ORIGIN" – IVAN PAVLOV

WHEN DOES THE PROBLEM OCCUR?

When does a problem occur? When did it occur? When was it first noticed? Does the problem occur at a particular time or in response to a trigger? How frequently does it occur? Is there a pattern that is causing concern? Could a problem emerge in the future?

The analysis of timing and frequency are crucial inputs for diagnosing a problem. In some cases, it could literally determine whether or not a solution can be devised. For example, if a problem seems to happen randomly and cannot be replicated, that can prevent an accurate diagnosis, hampering our search for a solution. The When question is all about time and timing: past, present, future; events, trends, frequency, and forecasts.

Since the symptom is noticed at a point in time, the first two questions are interconnected, and many times can be considered together.

"AWARENESS OF IGNORANCE IS THE BEGINNING OF WISDOM" – SOCRATES

WHERE IS THE PROBLEM HAPPENING?

Locating where the problem is happening is integral to problem-solving. Depending on the problem, this could be a geographic location, a division, a team, an individual, an organ, a system, process, function or component; or a combination of the above.

A natural extension of this question is: where is the problem originating from? In mechanical and even physiological systems like the human body, there can often be a distinction between the apparent location and the originating source.

This question can be expanded further to identify systems. This opens the door for *systems thinking* (which analyses interactions between systems) and lays the groundwork for the *How* question that will be asked later. A system is a group of things. Its components can be physical, logical or conceptual. In complex problems, multiple systems are involved and they interact dynamically. The human body for example has several systems: cardiovascular, lymphatic, skeletal and so on. A disease can impact multiple systems, in a very complex manner.

Be it troubleshooting a machine, examining a human, a personal crisis, an organizational problem or even assessing our position in a game of chess, locating the problem is a pre-requisite to solving it. Situating a problem within its broader context plays a key part in determining the focus and scope of the solution.

> *"YOU SEE, BUT YOU DO NOT OBSERVE" –*
> *SHERLOCK HOLMES*

WHO IS INVOLVED?

This question is about discovering who is impacted or involved; looking at the stakeholders involved. At a minimum, in any problem there is at least one person involved – the problem solver. Most problems will involve two or more stakeholders. Complex problems, particularly social or political ones, will typically require engaging a vast array of stakeholders, some of whom can have competing interests even!

A stakeholder is anyone impacted by the problem, in any way. Stakeholders can be individuals, groups, departments, entities, organizations, customers, suppliers or regulators even. They influence the solution and its implementation. They can also influence the problem. Indeed, in some cases, they may be a part of the problem itself. In all cases though, they will influence the solution. Understanding the motivations, emotions, aspirations, sentiments and experiences of stakeholders adds great depth to our analysis. It improves the fit of the solution, which in turn improves the solution acceptance and satisfaction.

> *"IT IS ONLY WITH THE HEART THAT ONE CAN SEE RIGHTLY" – ANTOINE DE SAINT-EXUPERY*

WHAT IS THE IMPACT?

This step is about sizing the problem. Depending on the problem, impact can be quantified in different ways. It could quite literally be a physical impact like an injury or collision, or something impacting an area. It could be the amount or extent of variation from a target condition, standard, or key performance indicator. It could also be financial impact, which is a common sizing mechanism. Dollar values can be measured tangibly and even be used to quantify "soft" or potential impacts like reputation or risk. Evaluating the tangible and intangible financial cost of a problem lies at the heart of most analyses.

QUANTIFICATION IS INTEGRAL TO PROBLEM SOLVING. It is important to be both precise and perceptive with quantification. Precision helps avoid overstating or understating the current situation. Perceptiveness helps avoid over-rating or under-estimating the future impact. Obtaining an accurate picture of the impact or "blast-radius" to use contemporary jargon, is essential to formulating our problem-solving approach. Having quantified the benefits, costs, and risks, we can answer a vital question that naturally follows an impact assessment: is the problem worth solving? If yes, then the next judgement will be around timing: at what point is an intervention necessary? In some cases, we may adopt a passive "wait-and-watch" approach until an imperative for action transpires. In the main however, we will usually take an active approach to problem solving. This is because most problems we face will usually be important, or urgent, or both; and hence require action.

Quantification provides the basis for deciding our overall stance on the problem. It is the most pivotal assessment in the discovery process.

> *"DUBITO, ERGO COGITO, ERGO SUM. I DOUBT, THEREFORE I THINK, THEREFORE I AM"* – RENE DESCARTES

WHY IS THE PROBLEM HAPPENING?

In his journal paper *From Data to Wisdom*[1], American Professor Russell Ackoff discussed the concepts of information and knowledge. Information, obtained by processing raw data, answers questions like who, what, where, when and how many. This information is used to build knowledge and understanding, which answer respectively, the *How* and *Why* questions. His framework is basis of the D-I-K-W (DATA-INFORMATION-KNOWLEDGE-WISDOM) PYRAMID which depicts these concepts in a hierarchy based on their levels of abstraction.

Within our context, we have worked through the information gathering. Now it is time to progress on to the knowledge and understanding aspects. Till now, we have built a picture of the problem. The crux of discovery however is to find the cause of the problem. Why did the problem occur? What caused it? How did the current situation unfold? *Why* relates to factors, reasons and causes. *How* relates to the dynamics between the factors or the manner in which something happens. *Why* and *How* represent our understanding and knowledge of a situation. The quality of the answers to these questions represents the extent to which we have grasped a problem.

Asking *Why* is a simple yet powerful way to discover the cause(s) of a problem. Being an open-ended question, it reveals avenues for further questioning, allowing us to conduct a comprehensive inquiry. *Why* questions can also be appended to each other to create a string of deeper probes. This is the premise behind the 5 WHYS technique which holds that asking why (up to) five times in succession can reveal root causes. For example, say an app is being developed and testing for a component fails.

- Why did testing fail? Due to a calculation error.
- Why? The formula had changed but was not mentioned in the specification.
- Why? The formula was not confirmed with stakeholders at the right time.

Asking *Why* reveals a deeper cause (stakeholder engagement) that was not initially apparent. CAUSE & EFFECT DIAGRAMS can also be used for root cause analysis. The principle however remains the same.

A problem can stem from a single root cause or have multiple underlying factors, that contribute equally, or unequally, to it. The key is to identify plausible causes and build a chain of enquiry, by asking *Why*, that leads to the source(s) of the problem.

Given the power of asking *Why*, it is important to ask it at the right time. If asked too early, there will not be enough context to make use of its full power. For this reason, it is presented at the end of the sequence – after we have obtained answers to the *what*, *where* *when*, *who* and *how* questions. The required information and knowledge are gathered first, before probing deeper to complete our understanding.

Understanding the background and any relevant mental models allows us to answer *How* and *Why* questions more effectively.

The background can provide valuable insights. While we may be new to a problem, the problem itself may not be new. It could be an existing problem. History plays a crucial role in the process of discovery, particularly for longstanding issues that predecessors may have tackled. Understanding the historical context, reviewing previously attempted solutions and being aware of past constraints – all lead to a more incisive analysis.

Mental models can also be relevant. A mental model is a framework for understanding something. These models, whether held individually or collectively, include the theories, concepts, heuristics, and axioms relevant to a particular domain or industry. Sometimes, a problem's root cause can trace back to a flawed mental model. What is (was) the prevailing mental model? Are any assumptions now outdated?

Grasping the reasons (why) and mechanisms (how) behind a problem is the essence of the discovery phase. Everything else builds upon this insight.

The challenge of discovery is to balance effort against results. While it is important to be thorough, it is prudent to not needlessly pursue discovery past the point of diminishing returns. The exact point will vary with the problem. It is about balance, a concept that we will discuss further in the Mindset chapter.

"NO PROBLEM CAN BE SOLVED FROM THE SAME LEVEL OF CONSCIOUSNESS THAT CREATED IT" – ALBERT EINSTEIN

WHAT IS IMPORTANT?

Asking *Why* is about gleaning insights. An insight implies depth of understanding. It can shed a new light on things or reveal an esoteric factor that changes how we view things. Insights empower us to revisit the problem in a more knowledgeable and enlightened state. They allow us to see what a problem is really about. For simple problems the discovery process will usually be short and there will be a manageable number of factors to allow us to determine the gist of a problem. As problems get more complicated, discovery will usually yield a lot of information. The information gathered will be of varying importance. To see the "forest from the trees", we need to distil the key factors of a problem, and, by doing so, filter out the "noise".

Using the phrase coined by engineer and quality management guru Joseph Juran, this step is about distinguishing the VITAL FEW FROM THE TRIVIAL MANY. Juran developed this concept based on the work of Italian engineer Vilfredo Pareto, whose research had discovered that 80% of the land in Italy was owned by 20% of the families[2]. Also known as Pareto's Law or the 80/20 rule, this aphorism of unequal distribution has a special role in analysis. The crux of any problem can be traced to a handful of crucial factors that wield a disproportionately large influence. By distilling these vital factors and addressing them specifically, we can solve the problem more efficiently and effectively.

Chess for example, involves rapid problem-solving cycles. Every move requires a quick analysis of where various threats or opportunities are, when, why and how they can arise, and what impact they can have. At each turn, players face multiple issues, but have only the one move. They have to distil what is important, and act accordingly.

This step is about synthesizing our analysis, findings and insights to determine the most influential factors. What is important? Answering this question lays the foundation to formulate the PROBLEM STATEMENT which is a concise factual description of the problem and its salient aspect(s).

"WHEN YOU HAVE ELIMINATED THE IMPOSSIBLE, WHATEVER REMAINS, HOWEVER IMPROBABLE, MUST BE THE TRUTH" – SHERLOCK HOLMES

METHOD: 7W+H

Problem solving happens in many capacities and contexts. We may be solving a personal problem, or be solving a problem as part of our job. In workplaces, there may be specialists who solve specific or more advanced problems. Some may solve technical problems; while others may solve strategic problems. Also, problems themselves can exist anywhere on the continuum between simple and complex. All of this has a bearing on the tools that are used. Some tools are specific to industries while others have gained cross-industry application.

Regardless of the context, certain fundamental questions guide the discovery process: What, Who, When, Where, Why, and How. Known as interrogative words in grammar, their literal function is to act as prompts for questions.

They are usually described by collective terms like 5Ws or 5W+H or the 6 HONEST MEN, a term coined by writer Rudyard Kipling, is probably the best and most memorable epithet for these faithful and competent allies in problem solving: "I KEEP SIX HONEST SERVING MEN (THEY TAUGHT ME ALL I KNEW); THEIR NAMES ARE WHAT AND WHY AND WHEN AND HOW AND WHERE AND WHO". The simplicity of these questions should not be mistaken for lack of potency. The directions they provide allow us to cover all relevant facets of a problem, in an intuitive, efficient and effective manner.

5W+H describes the foundational elements for any inquiry. It can be enriched by incorporating additional questions, particularly "What" questions. The term *what* is used to identify, describe or select something. Problem discovery can yield a lot of information. Asking "what" periodically helps in segmenting information, which makes analysis more effective.

This chapter uses 3 *What* questions. The very first one (what has come to our attention) describes the apparent problem. The second one (what is the impact) describes the magnitude of the problem. The very last one (what is important) distils the discovery enquiry into its most salient aspects. Start – Middle - End. What questions signpost the discovery process.

The remaining "W"s and "H" cover other dimensions: When (timing), Where (location), Who (entities), Why (causes), and How (ways).

The modified approach presented here can, very literally, be called the 7W+H METHOD. By working through these interrogative prompts, we cover all important facets of a problem. Progressing through them sequentially, as outlined in this chapter, allows for a systematic transition from gathering information through to knowledge and understanding. A visual summary is provided next. The list of 7W+H questions is also found in the Appendix 1.

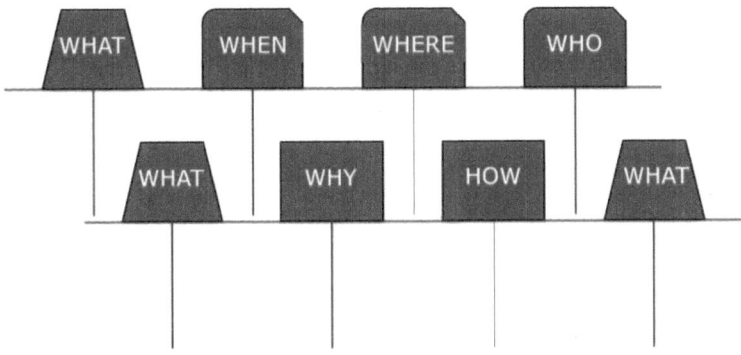

Figure 5: 7W+H

Σ

In terms of the problem-solving journey (articulated in the Map), the Discover step corresponds to the *Where are we now?* question. By the end of this step, we should be able to understand the current situation and the major drivers, causes or factors. Discovery should allow us to understand where we are, and why.

Problems relate to a discrepancy or distance from a target state. This step was about the current state. The next step will be about the desired or target state. Onwards we go!

HOLLAND CHOCOLATES

Holland Chocolates is a medium sized manufacturing company, that produces traditional chocolate. It has been in business for 15 years and done well. In the past few quarters however, profits have declined by 5% per quarter. An industry report also shows their market share down to 21% to 18%.

What should they do?

Problem-solving is about discrepancy and effort. There is a discrepancy. Correcting it requires effort.

The leadership team at Holland Chocolates must understand the problem, and devise a solution. They create a Map, and begin by assessing their current situation. Where are we currently? Why are we here?

They demarcate the symptoms: profits have declined by 5% quarter-on-quarter, which is the main concern; market share has dropped to 18%. In simpler problems, symptoms can point directly to the root cause. Recognizing the complexity of this issue, the team avoids jumping to conclusions and decides to investigate further.

The business operates in two divisions: consumer and commercial. After reviewing reports, the team discovers that while the commercial division is stable, the consumer division, particularly its core product line, has significantly dragged down overall profitability. The downward trend has persisted for three consecutive quarters, and if left unchecked, the $2 million shortfall will impact future investments and share value. Armed with this information, the team identifies the relevant stakeholders to solicit their inputs in to the problem.

The *what*, when, *where*, *who* questions have helped the team to scope the problem and identify its impact.

Having gathered sufficient information to develop good knowledge of the issue, the team now feel prepared to delve into understanding the deeper cause(s) – the *Why* and *How* of the problem.

The team decide to conduct a survey with a cross-section of stakeholders. It reveals that various factors have depressed profitability, including:

- Increased competition from local stores
- Rising costs of raw materials and energy
- Ageing equipment on core production line
- Inefficient production processes
- Staff turnover and shortages

- Product offerings (from the core production line) no longer satisfy modern consumer preferences

Most problems have a number of contributing factors. Not all factors are equal. Some are more prominent than others. The next, and final step of problem discovery, is to distil the most salient factor. To do this, they ask: *what is important here?*

The team plots the survey responses by frequency. The most prominent factor emerges: an outdated product line. As consumer preferences have shifted, Holland Chocolates' core products are perceived as old-fashioned, resulting in a significant drop in demand. This is the key driver of reduced profits.

Through an intuitive and structured problem discovery approach, the team have a clear understanding of:

- where they are (declining profits)
- and why (outdated product line *inter alia*)

They fill in the first quadrant of the Problem-Solving Canvas. The first step (Discovery) is complete.

The Smart Problem Solver

DEFINE THE GOAL

Chapter 5: What will success look like?

The Define step corresponds to the *Where do we want to be?* question on the Map. Its purpose is to define the goal and frame the problem in a way that helps us to best accomplish the goal. This is a crucial step in the problem-solving process. How well we understand the goal and how well we frame the problem correlates directly with how well we solve the problem.

Definition is the fulcrum of problem solving. The task on hand is to absorb the insights and frame the problem in a way that solves it effectively. For simple problems, this step can be quite obvious. For complex problems, it requires deeper thinking, and iteration.

"LUCK IS WHERE OPPORTUNITY MEETS PREPARATION" – SENECA

WHAT IS OUR ACTIONABLE GOAL STATEMENT?

THE GOAL REPRESENTS A TARGET WE WISH TO ACHIEVE. It is our definition of what success looks like. It can be a measure or metric like dollars, scores or key performance indicators. It can be an obligation, a deliverable, a target condition or a target behaviour.

For some problems, the goal may be known from the outset of the problem. This is particularly true for problems in the "gap from standard" genre, where the problem is caused due to a discrepancy from a target measure. For other problems, the goal may not be known at the outset. We may want to derive, or specify it based on the analysis and insights gained from the discovery process. Regardless, now is the time to review, revise or define the goal.

This is also a good time to gain clarity about what is not the goal. What is not in scope? What is not broken? Are there any inadmissible actions? What is not the case? By articulating the contrapositive case, these questions remove ambiguity, provide direction and hence allow us to define the goal with greater precision. A clearly defined goal is invaluable for solution design.

A good goal statement is:

- FOCUSSED. It must relate to the problem.
- SPECIFIC. It must provide clear direction for solution design.
- MEASURABLE. It must be measurable either qualitatively or quantitatively, so that we can evaluate the success of our solution after it has been deployed.
- NEITHER BROAD NOR NARROW. It must have the right level of granularity to be effective. If too broad, it may not translate into meaningful action or prove to be beyond the influence of the problem-solver(s). If too narrow, the solution may be sub-optimal and unduly constrained, leaving limited flex for creativity or unexpected situations.

Determining the right scope is a balancing act. There cannot be any prescription for the "right" level of granularity, as it depends entirely on the context. If in doubt, it is best to start with something slightly broader that is challenging yet achievable. Broader statements leave more avenues for innovative problem solving, and indeed sometimes, can even make us re-interpret the problem in a new light. It is better to start broader and then scope down, if required, than trying to grow out of the tiny box that overly narrow statements lead us into.

Just as importantly, a goal statement must be ACTIONABLE. The goal is the bridge that helps us transition from the problem realm towards the solution realm, from problem discovery to solution design. To facilitate this, we need to adopt an active and forward-looking perspective of what we can do to solve the problem. To accomplish this, we need to re-frame the goal as an action item. For this, we need to weave insights gained during discovery, into an actionable statement that guides the solution.

By framing the problem and goal as an opportunity for action, we mentally orient ourselves for better solution design. Problem solving is a process. The outputs of one step are the inputs of the subsequent step. Having a high-quality and tailored input, allows us to perform the subsequent activity better. Defining the actionable goal statement is the pivotal step in the problem-solving. The frame we develop here will guide our subsequent thinking and actions.

Framing can have very profound outcomes. The Gordian Knot is a prime example, an impossibly complex knot tied to a chariot. It was prophesied that the person who unravelled the knot would become the ruler of Asia. Many attempted to untie the knot in the usual way and failed. Alexander the Great approached the problem differently. Rather than untying the knot, he sliced through it with his sword, effectively achieving the desired result—the knot's removal.

The action statement can take many forms. It can come in guises and names like opportunity statement, or design challenge, each differing with the context and methodology. Ideally, it should be articulated in a manner, and language, that is best understood by the problem-solver(s). While there is no agreed or prescribed structure for it, the HOW MIGHT WE format provides a great scaffolding to build the actionable goal statement.

> "A PROBLEM WELL-STATED IS A PROBLEM-HALF SOLVED" – CHARLES KETTERING

METHOD: HOW MIGHT WE?

How Might We (HMW) is a framing technique, popularized by design firm IDEO as part of its *Design Thinking* methodology[3]. It rephrases problems and insights as opportunities for design by adding "How

Might We" in the beginning. If we break down *HMW*; the interrogative adverb HOW turns it into a question, and the modal verb MIGHT, implies possibility (similar to using could *vs.* should).

The value of using this technique is that it poses the goal as a question or challenge to be addressed. Doing so, puts us into an inquisitive state of mind. Solution development benefits greatly from divergent[4] or broad, creative thinking. By being inquisitive, we naturally set ourselves up for divergent thinking. This prevents us from jumping straight to pet solutions, without having considered at least some alternative(s).

HMW is a prefix for articulating the design challenge. I like to use a hybrid approach that merges this prefix with the key parameters of the problem to give the actionable goal statement. To the HMW prefix, we append an action verb (e.g., make, improve etc.), the goal, and then, as required, qualify it with attributes or qualities that are critical to the outcome we seek. The operative term is critical. How do we know what is critical? We derive it from the indicators, needs, insights, causes or drivers of the problem identified during discovery (*what is important?*).

To illustrate, consider the following problem. Say we have an ageing car with some repair issues. Our problem discovery has shown that best and most economic course of action is to replace it. What to replace it with, that is up for consideration. Our goal statement could look like:

- *How Might We replace our existing car with a modern and reliable car?*

The HMW frame has made this statement sound more "open". It is now a question rather than a prescription like "I need a new car". Compared to imperatives, questions provide a much better basis for ideation.

THE GOAL IS NOT THE SOLUTION. IT IS THE RESULT THE SOLUTION WILL DELIVER. By asking HMW, we mentally prepare ourselves to solve the problem. Without this optimistic and open-ended framing, we can very easily go down the route of simply wrapping a solution as a goal statement. The goal of replacing the car is then qualified with key attributes – reliable and modern car. To reduce ambiguity, we can define some MEASURES for parameters like reliable (e.g., no repair issues, reliable brand) and modern (e.g., 2022+ models). Measures are important. If we do not have a way to measure success, we will not know whether we have been successful. Depending on our goal, whether we are working towards a target state, score, indicator, condition or behaviour, the measure can be quantitative, qualitative, single or composite. HMW is an enabler. The key is to articulate the goal in a manner that is focused enough to provide direction, flexible enough to allow an unprejudiced search for solutions, and measurable enough to verify success.

Σ

The Define step corresponds to the *Where do we want to be?* question. By the end of this step, we should have defined the goal and obtained a general direction for working on the solution. This marks the half-way stage of our problem-solving endeavour. From here onwards, our journey will focus on the solution. We are ready to chart out our course of action. Time to get our (creative) thinking caps on!

HOLLAND CHOCOLATES

Holland Chocolates have a gap relative to the expected profits for the quarter. The goal in this case is to restore profitability levels. Using the insights gained from the Discovery phase, the leadership team at Holland Chocolates develops the actionable goal statement and comes up with:

- How Might We redesign our product line so that it's contemporary, and profitable.

They goal statement provides sufficient direction for solution design without prescribing a solution, has the right scope, and addresses the root cause.

Goal statements are the bridge between problem phases (Discover -Define) and the solution phases (Devise -Deploy). They force us to think, and re-think about the real problem, and the parameters of the solution that will solve the problem most effectively. Iterating over an actionable goal statement is common and an important part of the problem-solving process.

It's common to iterate through HMW statements until a suitable one is reached. For illustration, here are some statements that Holland Chocolates rejected:

- *HMW introduce melon-chocolate, the most profitable flavour in the market?* It's too specific and resembles a solution dressed up as a goal. It may end up being the solution, but why preclude other options so early?
- *HMW improve profits?* It's too broad.
- *HMW reduce fixed costs to improve profits?* Too specific, and does not solve any known root cause.
- *HMW stop making losses on this product line?* This is technically fine, but framing it optimistically is better for ideation.

The team writes the HMW statement in the second quadrant of their Problem-Solving Canvas. They have an actionable goal statement, and a clear rationale for choosing it. The second step (Define) is complete.

DEVISE THE SOLUTION
Chapter 6: How can we solve the problem?

The Devise step corresponds to the *How can we get there?* question on the Map. The first two questions on the Map were about orientation (and hence began with *where*). The last two questions are about navigation (and begin with a *How*). A *How* question typically leads towards details, strategies, tactics and mechanics. Using the goal statement as a basis, the task on hand in this step is to generate ideas and from these ideas, select the best candidate.

This is the creative step of problem solving that brings together everything we have learnt about the problem so far to craft a suitable solution. For simpler problems, the range of solutions can be limited or quite obvious even. For complex problems, there are typically many routes for achieving the solution. Regardless of the type of problem, the interrogations will follow a three-step pattern: generate ideas on how the solve the problem, develop decision-making criteria, and select the idea that best fits the criteria.

> *"HE WHO HAS A WHY TO LIVE CAN BEAR ALMOST ANY HOW" – FRIEDRICH NIETZSCHE*

WHAT ARE SOME IDEAS TO PURSUE?

THE SOLUTION MAY BE A PRODUCT, A SERVICE, A REPAIR, A PURCHASE, OR A COURSE OF ACTION. Conventional solutions arrive to us naturally. However, it is important to not limit ourselves to conventional solutions only. A creative, innovative or unexpected idea may actually lead to the best solution. In the goal statement, we left some scope for creativity. Now is the time to engage in divergent thinking and undertake a broad exploration of possible solutions. At the initial stage, quantity is important. Any idea that addresses the goal statement must be entertained – including those that seem far-fetched or radical. The best ideas will be shortlisted later. Initially, we should go for quantity. A pitfall to avoid here is pursuing pet solutions or predetermined ones without sufficiently considering (any) other alternatives. Except for very simple or well-established problems which may have an obvious solution, a broad idea-generation exercise improves the quality of the solution. Creative thinking challenges the notions we may have about the solution, or the problem even. It makes us think more critically; and critical thinking is a mindset that is central to smart problem solving.

There are a number of techniques to foster creative thinking. SCAMPER is one of the more popular ones and particularly useful in problems requiring product or service design. The acronym represents seven ways in which we can rethink the existing situation. It stands for[5]: Substitute – Combine – Adapt – Modify – Put to Another Use – Eliminate – Reverse. By rethinking or re-framing, the core attributes of a problem along these axes, we can devise some crafty solutions. Take the ageing car that we want to replace. The conventional solution would be to replace it with another car. However, if we substitute one aspect (ownership) for another (non-ownership) or one term (car) for its super-set term (mobility), new solutions transpire. Car lease options are now becoming widespread, acceptable and affordable. They provide well-maintained cars and have newer models. The lease option could be an idea to consider. From a problem-solving perspective, this example shows two things. First is the importance of articulating the goal at a level that allows flex space for varied solutions to emerge. The second is that by viewing a problem as a series of components that can be arranged and rearranged like modular building blocks, we can use the very parameters of the problem to devise creative solutions. Creative thinking challenges our existing mental models and encourages us to develop new ones. Approaching a problem with a new or revised mental model can lead to radically effective and transformational solutions. Disruptive innovations like AirBnB, Uber or iPhone have all centred on reimaging products, services and situations using new mental models.

During discovery, we explored the problem from various angles. Now, we are exploring the (possible) solution from various angles. We adopted a discerning and analytical mindset to understand the problem. In the Define phase, we need to adopt the same critical mindset to evaluate assumptions and constraints. Assumptions are ever-present. Sometimes we may be conscious of them. For most part, they are latent and need to be fished out. By explicitly surfacing our assumptions, and challenging them, we open up our minds to fresh perspectives and insights. Same goes for constraints. Many times, the constraints are not as "hard" as they seem and equally, many times seemingly "soft" constraints can be quite binding in reality. By thinking creatively and critically, we can cover a wide range of options: from conventional ones to far-fetched ones; and even surface ideas hiding behind cognitive curtains of assumptions and constraints.

Considering a broad range of ideas does more than just improve our chances of finding a great solution. It can also lead us towards solving a bigger problem. Solving problems at a larger scale can often lead to robust and elegant solutions that also cascade down to smaller problems. This is the premise behind GOOGLE'S 10X THINKING which holds that innovation happens when you try to improve a situation 10 times instead of just by 10 percent[6]. Depending on the situation, it is well worth considering solving a bigger version of the problem at hand. At best, we will be successful and have a more impactful solution. At worst, some of the ideas gained can be used to solve the existing problem.

> "WHENEVER I RUN INTO A PROBLEM I CAN'T SOLVE, I ALWAYS MAKE IT BIGGER. I CAN NEVER SOLVE IT BY TRYING TO MAKE IT SMALLER, BUT IF I MAKE IT BIG ENOUGH, I CAN BEGIN TO SEE THE OUTLINES OF A SOLUTION" – DWIGHT D EISENHOWER

WHAT ARE OUR CRITERIA?

We have explored various ideas. Now we need to reduce the number of options and converge on the idea with the best fit. The first step in doing this is to define some decision-criteria. Having criteria is an important part of structured problem solving. Without criteria, it is not possible to compare objectively or consistently.

The actionable goal statement acts like the overarching scope and filter for idea generation, especially if any qualifiers are stipulated. Additional selection criteria can also be derived from the insights gleaned during problem-discovery. They may even come to light during solution exploration! Problem-solving is rarely linear. New realizations can transpire at any time, and we have to remain adaptable, while keeping the overall picture in mind. This is the theme of the Dynamic Mindset, which is explored later.

The importance of developing good evaluation criteria should not be under-estimated. It has a direct impact on the solution we will select and therefore the outcome that we will need to live with. Problem-solving steps build on each other. A good discovery exercise, a crisp goal definition and a broad search for solutions will help us select insightful criteria, which will result in a more impactful solution.

Good evaluation criteria have two characteristics. They are applicable or relevant to all the alternatives. If a criterion is only relevant for some alternatives and not others, it can hinder equitable evaluation. They are also manageable or limited to a reasonable quantity. A good rule of thumb is to have 3 – 5 key criteria. This falls within the MAGIC NUMBER 7 theory[7] which holds that humans can store 7±2 items in their short-term memory. For some problems, assigning a weight or relative importance to each criterion can also be beneficial. This facilitates the selection of ideas that score highly on more critical criteria and reduces the likelihood of tied results.

In the main, it is best to start with a limited set of *key* criteria as this surfaces the main decision-making points while not resulting in a cognitive overload. Sub-criteria can then be added as required. In the

Discover step, we talked about the Pareto principle. The same concept applies here: distinguishing the vital few from the trivial many. Discover and Devise phases are in effect mirror images. The only difference is that one focusses on exploring the problem while the other focusses on exploring the solution. The essence and mental thought processes are the same: using divergent thinking to gather information and then employing convergent thinking to distil the most salient elements.

> *"IT IS NOT ENOUGH TO DO YOUR BEST; YOU MUST KNOW WHAT TO DO, AND THEN DO YOUR BEST"* –
> WILLIAM EDWARDS DEMING

WHAT IS THE BEST SOLUTION?

The best solution is the one that best meets our needs. Insightful research, clarity about the goal, an actionable goal statement, a broad search for solutions and concise criteria. When all these are in place, the solution will transpire as a matter of course. This is the power of adopting a structured approach. It provides a path that weaves in rigour with structure and leads sequentially, yet seamlessly, from symptom to solution. Structured approaches are repeatable and extensible. They can be applied and re-applied across a range to contexts. When we solve problems using a structured approach, we gain a multiplier. Not only do we get better at solving problems, we also get a repeatable method that allows us to keep getting better at solving problems.

THE SOLUTION IS OUR STRATEGY TO REACH THE GOAL. It answers the Map question of *How can we get there?* To make our problem solving more effective, we need to be clear on the reason for choosing our solution. Why will we get there in this way? What is the rationale behind our solution strategy? These questions provide mental reaffirmation for the rationale behind the decision we are going to make. Being able to explain why a solution was selected also proves useful during implementation, particularly when multiple stakeholders are involved and the decision-maker is answerable to them.

Decision-making is tied intricately to problem-solving. Selecting the solution is the most pivotal decision in problem-solving. A problem spans two horizons: past-present – where it occurs, and present-future, where it is solved. It's important to look forward when deciding on solutions. If we don't, the pitfall of the SUNK COST FALLACY might await us. Sunk costs[8] are costs that have been incurred in the past, and cannot be recovered. They are *sunk*, irreversibly, and as such should not be allowed to skew future decision-making. Future decisions should only be guided by future gains and losses. To illustrate, say Bob pays and is offered a $10 flat rate for all products, as opposed to the regular $25 retail price. Despite nothing catching his interest, Bob feels compelled to "recoup" some value from his visit and purchases a $10 item he doesn't need. The initial $50 is a sunk cost and should not influence the decision to buy the $10. This throwing of "good money after bad" when it is better to cut our losses is the essence of the sunk cost fallacy. It's a common error that has led to significant losses, particularly in product or systems development where more resources are poured into trying to salvage failing projects instead of accepting the loss and shifting focus. The value of a decision should be based on current reality, and not on investments (cost, time or effort) that were made in the past – and cannot now be recovered.

A decision is made at a point in time. It is based on inputs like the information available, the intention, and the logic applied - at that point in time. Various factors influence decisions; and decisions influence results. Many times, however, we fall victim to OUTCOME BIAS, which is a cognitive tendency to judge the quality of a decision purely on the end result while ignoring the contributing factors[9]. When judging results, we must evaluate holistically the underlying reasons, processes[10] and decisions that led to the results. In the next step (Deploy), the final activity will be to evaluate the success of our problem-solving endeavour. One of the inputs into that evaluation will be the rationale for our strategy – what was the process, thinking or reason for reaching the solution in that way, as opposed to any other way. By reviewing the rationale for our selected solution before finalizing it, we create a logical audit trail of our decision-making. This proves useful later for tracing results back to our actions and decisions.

Devising solutions is a crucial step in the problem-solving process. The challenge of this phase is balancing creativity and sentimentality with pragmatism. While it is important to be creative, we must at some point, draw the line between idealism and pragmatism, and reconsider the value of pursuing solutions that are unattainable. The solution must be fit-for-purpose and pragmatic. The Desirable-

Feasible-Viable method, discussed next, is one way to achieve this.

> *"THE MAIN THING IS TO KEEP THE MAIN THING THE MAIN THING" – STEPHEN COVEY*

METHOD: DESIRABLE-FEASIBLE-VIABLE

The design firm IDEO has popularised *Design Thinking*, which they define as a human-centred approach to innovation that integrates the needs of people with the possibilities of technology and commercial success.

IDEO's classic[11] three-circle Venn diagram showing Desirability, Feasibility and Viability, with *Design Thinking* living at the intersection of these three attributes, is a great technique for evaluating design decisions. The ideal solution will sit at the intersection of the three circles. It will be "humanly desirable" *and* "technologically feasible" *and* "economically viable".

In a problem-solving context, these attributes can be (re)interpreted as:

- DESIRABLE: Is it an appealing solution?
- FEASIBLE: Is it realistic? Can it actually be done?
- VIABLE: Is it economical? Will it work out?

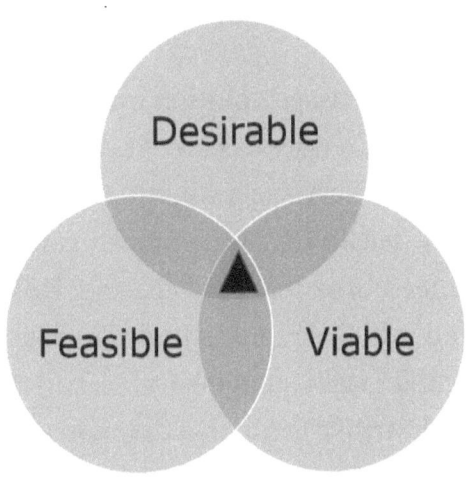

Figure 6: Desirable-Feasible-Viable

Do I/we want it? Can I/we have it? Will it work out? These are essential questions to consider when making decisions. An idea being considered must exhibit some merit in each attribute. If an idea is desirable and viable but not feasible, then it literally cannot be implemented. Similarly, if an idea is feasible and desirable but not viable, it will not be sustainable. An idea must have some degree of desirability, feasibility, and viability, and conversely, it must not lack completely in any of these aspects. Desirable-Feasible-Viable (DFV) enables a holistic evaluation of an idea or solution. It ensures that idea(s) being taken forward will have a robust foundation for success.

Previously, we discussed solution criteria. In situations where no criteria exist or don't readily come to mind, DFV can serve as a substitute. The attributes of desirability, feasibility, and viability can also be integrated into a broader set of criteria. DFV can also be used as an initial screening tool. The idea(s) deemed feasible, viable and desirable, can then be distinguished further through a detailed analysis of pros and cons, or by employing tie-breaking criteria.

The Devise step is about finding the most complete solution to the problem we are facing. DFV is an insightful, practical and multi-dimensional tool for assessing ideas or the selected solution.

The next step (Deploy) is about implementation. Having holistically verified the desirability, feasibility and viability of the solution beforehand, we can roll-out the solution more perceptively and confidently.

Σ

We entered this step with the goal statement. Based on that, we generated alternatives, devised selection criteria and selected the best solution. At the end of this step, we should know our preferred solution, and be clear on the rationale for pursuing that solution. Selecting the solution, is a decisive moment in a problem-solving endeavour. Having done this, we find ourselves standing at the threshold of the most important step of all – deploying the solution. Till now, the journey had a strong analytical flavour. The next step will be all about action. Staying with that metaphor, we are now ready to get into the car and drive to our destination. Put the keys in the ignition and fasten your seatbelts!

HOLLAND CHOCOLATES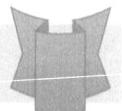

Having established the actionable problem statement, the team at Holland Chocolates starts exploring solutions and comes up with a list of ideas. They now need to select the best idea for implementation.

While they may complement it later with a detailed list of weighted criteria, the team decide use the DFV method to rank their 3 shortlisted ideas.

- Idea A involves introducing new organic products and flavours produced on existing equipment.
- Idea B involves launching new products but only after an overhaul of processes and machinery.
- Idea C wants to address this situation through corporate acquisitions.

A minimal level of change, and fast time to market makes Idea A feasible, desirable and viable.

Idea B is feasible but requires investment and has a delayed time-to-market. Since it addresses the problems of product offerings and ageing equipment, it's more comprehensive, which increases its desirability.

Idea C has low feasibility but otherwise, makes for an expedient solution. Since it's not possible to do in the present circumstances, it's not pursued any further.

Using DFV ensures that the idea(s) taken forward are robust across all three aspects, and have an inherent foundation for success. Finer criteria can be applied later to differentiate or prioritize further.

Ideas A and B are equally credible. They are feasible, viable and desirable in their own right. The challenge is to choose which one is comparatively better. Except for simple cases, there will rarely be any one perfect solution. Every solution will have pros and cons. The one with the best overall suitability, given the present circumstances, ought to be chosen.

The team revisit the goal statement to see if they can identify a tie-break criterion like strategic vision, risk appetite or time to market. They also consult with stakeholders to find out what is important to consider.

Let's say, Idea B is finally chosen.

The team updates the Problem-Solving Canvas with the solution, and their rationale for choosing it. The third step (Define) is complete.

DEPLOY THE SOLUTION
Chapter 7: Is the problem solved?

We have done the analysis, made our decision and selected the solution. The Deploy step is where the rubber hits the road. It is where the solution is brought to life. In terms of the Map, the Define step answered the question: *How can we get there?* Using the journey metaphor and with the actual "drive" to the destination being implied, the Deploy step corresponds to the *How will we know we are there?* question. The solution is the means to solve the problem. Did we solve the problem - and how do we know? At the start of our problem-solving endeavour, an indicator, realization or symptom alerted us to a problem. We then defined a goal and devised a solution. At the end, after deploying the solution, we need to confirm that the problem has indeed been solved. With this, we come full-circle in our problem-solving endeavour.

A solution can be actualized in many ways. It can involve a purchase, an investment, a campaign, a project, new product, new software, a fix, repair or a course of action to meet the goal. In some cases, and especially for complex problems, like a pandemic, the solution may be a bouquet of actions or interventions put together to combat the problem. In all cases though, it will involve some action or activity. The interrogations of this step focus on action planning and post-implementation evaluation.

> *"IN PREPARING FOR BATTLE I HAVE ALWAYS FOUND THAT PLANS ARE USELESS, BUT PLANNING IS INDISPENSABLE" – DWIGHT D EISENHOWER*

WHAT IS OUR ACTION PLAN?

To successfully implement solutions, it is important to have a robust plan and a system to monitor execution against the plan. This is typically achieved via the use of activity plans. At a minimum, activity plans contain the task, and basic execution details (who, when). This format can be expanded upon depending on the situation. For delivering bigger solutions, we may require a full-scale project plan which will show the scope, schedule, dependencies and resourcing. An activity plan should be prepared for every solution we implement, with the level of detail adjusted according to the situation. Activity plans are covered later in the Method section.

Good idea but poor execution. All of us can recall exasperating experiences where this has been the case. No matter how much merit a solution has, if it is not implemented properly, it won't achieve the desired impact. The challenge of this step is ensuring that the integrity and impact of the solution is not diminished by its implementation.

A solution may introduce a new product that people need to adapt to. It could introduce a new way of doing things, a new course of action or a new reality. Implementing any solution brings change. Change impacts people. Managing the human aspect is critical. Depending on the scope and setting of the problem, it could range from a simple conversation to formal stakeholder engagement, communications, change management, training and transition. The importance of change and stakeholder management should never be underestimated. It is often a crucial differentiator between success and failure, particularly for complex or sensitive problems. A solution may also not be implemented immediately. Sometimes, we may want to run a "test" before roll-out. This is a common practice in product or software design where solutions are piloted or prototyped before launch. Sometimes we may want to implement in steps or phases. In such situations, it becomes important to plan for the implementation *and* the transitory activities leading to it.

In the ageing car problem, let us say we decided to buy a new electric car. Implementing this solution is more than just a purchase. We have to decide when to purchase it, and equally how to sell the ageing car. We may also need to decide on a trade-in or finance option. Then comes the human side – how will the vehicle users, including granny Alice, adjust to the new car? Large or small, hard or soft, there are details to be worked through. The implementation plan must contain all the key activities required to bring a solution to life, along with those that help manage the change that the solution is about to (inevitably) introduce.

> *"THE SECRET OF CHANGE IS TO FOCUS ALL OF YOUR ENERGY, NOT ON FIGHTING THE OLD, BUT BUILDING ON THE NEW" – SOCRATES*

HOW TO CONFIRM SUCCESS?

We have deployed the solution. Problem solved then? Yes, but there is one more thing to do. A solution is the strategy for achieving the goal. Has the strategy worked? Did we achieve the goal? Did we solve the problem? Has the desired state been accomplished? These questions take us to the final inquiry of our problem-solving endeavour – how to verify success?

To answer this, we need to review the goal statement and evaluate whether the results achieved are as per the condition or measure(s) that we had desired. For simple problems and those involving troubleshooting or purely quantitative measures, verification can be straightforward. For more complex problems or those with intangible outcomes, it can take time to conclusively ascertain the success of the solution.

Evaluation "closes the loop" for our problem-solving endeavour. It confirms whether or not we have solved the problem - and to what degree. More importantly, it provides feedback on the efficacy of our methods. We can use the lessons learnt to solve future problems, or in the scenario where the solution did not fully solve the problem, we can use our evaluation to initiate targeted remedial action.

Structured problem-solving skills improve with practice. They are accumulative and transferrable. Through deliberate and regular evaluation of our problem-solving efforts, we can slowly build a mental database, that is rich and can be used repeatedly. It is precisely this capability that allows us to become more efficient and effective problem-solvers on a consistent basis.

"UNLESS COMMITMENT IS MADE, THERE ARE ONLY PROMISES AND HOPES; BUT NO PLANS" – PETER F DRUCKER

METHOD: ACTIVITY PLANS

An Activity Plan can be something as simple as an action list or task list. To be effective, an Activity Plan should include three basic pieces of information: WHAT, WHEN, WHO. What is the task? When will it be done? By whom? The resource and time (who and when), are important for assigning responsibility and tracking. A task list in itself is not a plan unless it is supplemented by resource and time information. Task, Time, and Person. This is the gist of an activity plan. It contains the activities required to deliver or realize the solution in a specific and tangible manner, along with the person responsible and a time-frame for action, and completion.

Activity planning leads naturally into the discipline of Project Management. For more complicated activities, we can use project management tools like Gantt charts to show schedules in much more detail and use other visualizations to analyse dependencies or resourcing. Project management is more than just schedule management. The widely referenced PRINCE2 project management methodology, talks about SIX VARIABLES[12] that need to be controlled in a project: time, cost, scope, quality, benefits and risk. These six variables efficaciously condense the balancing act (and art) of project management.

In professional situations, we will often use project management techniques to implement a solution. In personal situations it may seem like "overkill" to use project management concepts. However, adopting a structured approach always helps. A basic activity plan (what, who, when) and even a quick mental jog through the six variables can help us create simple yet effective plans of action for any activity, be it at work or at home.

When the implementation period is long, as it usually is for complex problems, things can also change in the meantime. That is something to be alert to, plan for, and solve cohesively. The Mindset section, coming up next, discusses this.

Σ

We entered this step with a solution in mind and made an action plan to realise it. By the end of this step, we should have deployed our solution and thereby solved the problem. After verifying that the problem has indeed been solved, we should give ourselves a deserved pat on the back. Our journey is now complete. Using a structured approach to successfully solve a problem is very fulfilling. It gives us a confidence boost for tackling other problems. Problems then, instead of being a daunting task, become a duel we relish, safe in the knowledge that we have the robust methodology to solve them.

This book centres on the Map-Model-Mindset methodology. The Map allowed us to visualize problem solving using the metaphor of a journey. Corresponding to the Map, the Model provided a structured process for solving problems. The next chapter discusses the third component: Mindset.

HOLLAND CHOCOLATES

Having decided on the solution, the team get into implementation mode. A project is created, complete with the plan of *who* will do *what*, *when*. At the end of the project, they anticipate having better equipment, better processes and a modern product offering.

The project will take time to deliver. The project team however is clear on their tasks, knows the solution, and the rationale for choosing it. Should any challenges or re-litigation emerge, the team will be well poised to respond accordingly, and cohesively.

In gap-from-target situations, monitoring is fairly self-defined. Post project, the team will monitor financials, sales data and market share to evaluate how successful their problem-solving effort has been.

The action plan is written in the fourth quadrant of the Problem-Solving Canvas. After the solution is implemented, they will share this one-pager with the Board to show their successful problem-solving journey, and place a celebratory green tick on it. ✓

THE PROBLEM-SOLVER'S MINDSET

Chapter 8: Being more potent

There is a fundamental structure common to all problems. As a corollary, there is also a fundamental approach that can be used for solving problems. This approach was presented in the Model. To get the most out this process, we need to increase our personal capability in problem solving. There are ways of thinking which we can adopt to become more potent problem-solvers. This chapter presents the 3 mindsets that accentuate problem-solving capabilities.

""THE WHOLE IS MORE THAN THE SUM OF ITS PARTS" – ARISTOTLE

CRITICAL THINKING

Critical thinking is an assembly of many analytical and logical skills. At its heart lies the critical mindset which involves questioning simultaneously both the reality that presents itself, and our own limitations in interpreting that reality. It is about being inquisitive, perceptive, sceptical and reflective to obtain maximum clarity on a situation. Using the journey metaphor, it is like driving. Our default view is the windscreen. To broaden our perspective and overcome our vision limitations, there is a rear-view mirror. There are also side-mirrors and on top of that we also turn our neck to physically view something that the side-mirrors may have missed. This is an example of the critical mindset where we cross-check our views to obtain an accurate picture.

CRITICAL THINKING IS ABOUT BEING DISCERNING. Instead of taking things at face value, it is about analysing, questioning and evaluating something before we accept it, and indeed, even after we have accepted it, in case new information changes our understanding[13]. Two aspects of critical thinking with particular relevance to problem solving are noted succinctly in Stella Cottrell's excellent book[14] *Critical Thinking Skills:* the ability to reflect sceptically and the ability to think in a reasoned way. Healthy constructive scepticism is about keeping an open mind on all possibilities and questioning continually to ascertain the (level of) truth of a situation or issue at hand. Thinking in a reasoned way involves having a rationale for our beliefs, being aware of it, and corroborating it through critical analysis of our beliefs. Critical thinking is about being perceptive and thoughtful. It is the differentiating quality of smart problem-solvers.

While critical thinking applies to all problem-solving steps, it finds particular application in the Discover and Define steps - when we are analysing the problem and when we are devising the solution. A critical assessment of the problem allows us to distil the material factors. This gives us confidence that we are headed in the right direction with respect to our search for a solution. An open-minded search and critical evaluation of ideas then gives us further confidence that our solution will be fit for purpose. Discover and Define are two pivotal steps in the problem-solving process. By employing critical thinking in these steps, we introduce analytical rigour at the two points in the process that require it most.

The Critical Mindset is about being inquisitive and probing, and putting our beliefs, understanding, hypotheses and assumptions to a thorough test before ascertaining their merit. It is about due diligence before accepting something.

In a problem-solving context, the purpose of critical thinking is to ensure (the highest possible) fidelity. Fidelity here means having a clear, perceptive, and unadorned view of a situation. When we truly grasp a problem, there will be high fidelity between reality and our understanding of it. Problems defined with high-fidelity lend themselves to elegant solutions.

Perhaps fittingly, the essence of critical analysis may be distilled into the question: *Am I asking the right questions?* Deriving the right answers to the right questions. This is the holy grail of problem-solving.

> "THE FIRST PRINCIPLE IS THAT YOU MUST NOT FOOL YOURSELF, AND YOU ARE THE EASIEST PERSON TO FOOL." – RICHARD FEYNMAN

BALANCE

THE AIM OF PROBLEM SOLVING IS TO SOLVE THE PROBLEM. The thing that matters most is the solution – the implemented solution to be precise. Preparation is done to facilitate execution. While we don't want to be under-prepared, we also don't want to spend time over-preparing, especially if it comes at the expense of execution. Balance is important. It is about exerting the *right* effort at each stage so that we keep the wheels moving on our overall problem-solving journey.

Imbalance arises from two factors. The first is not giving each problem-solving step its due importance. Each step in the problem-solving process prepares us analytically and psychologically for the next. Skipping steps, jumping to conclusions, pursuing pre-conceived notions without fully understanding the problem, all these cause imbalance and lead to sub-optimal and ill-fitting solutions. The second factor relates to the concept of diminishing returns which states that beyond a point, additional input only yields progressively smaller and diminishing returns. Over-analysis, over-precision, or dwelling on one step for too long are typical examples here.

The Balance Mindset is about apportioning our time and effort in a way that best supports the achievement of our ultimate goal – to solve the problem. It is about seeing the overall process (and progress), while being in the process. This mindset is encapsulated by the question: *Am I making progress towards the goal?* Smart problem solvers are thorough but also work through all the problem-solving steps in a steady and pragmatic manner.

> "LIFE IS LIKE RIDING A BICYCLE. TO KEEP YOUR BALANCE, YOU MUST KEEP MOVING" – ALBERT EINSTEIN

DYNAMISM

We live in a constant and ever-changing world. Naturally then, we also solve problems in a dynamic environment. We solve problems in a continuum of time. A problem comes to our attention at a point in time. The solution is produced at a later point in time. In between there is passage of time. Time exerts a dynamic influence on problem solving. It can change the nature of the problem or our understanding of it, or both. For simple problems that can be solved quickly, time may not introduce any material change. For more complex problems, time will play a part. The problem can change with time, the problem-solver's thinking can change with time. The solution may also need to change if the intervening time period has introduced some new information, realization or technology.

The problem-solving process must account for the time factor. We cannot change time. We cannot control time. The only option is to embrace this dynamism by being flexible and adaptable. To do this effectively, the problem-solving process must build in a mechanism for traceability. This way if something changes due to time, we can refer back to our original thinking to make comparisons or evaluate results. The simplest way to build traceability is being aware of, and clear about, the rationale for our thinking. By doing this, we create logical checkpoints. When something changes, we can go back through the chain of logic and adjust accordingly. For this reason, in the Problem-Solving Canvas, a *Why* question is referenced centrally by each component.

With the exception of simple problems, the problem-solving process is rarely linear. It is iterative because the context, and the knowledge, insights and experience of the problem-solver may evolve, while the problem is being solved. Particularly with complex problems, there is a (good) chance of oscillation between different problem-solving steps. To maintain the integrity of structured problem-solving, it is important to embrace iteration and change, and be poised to respond dynamically to it. Astute problem-solvers build mechanisms to cascade and reconcile changes in a coherent and cohesive manner.

The first two steps (Discover, Define) are about analysis and preparation. The latter two steps (Devise-Deploy) are about decision-making and execution. If something changes materially in the first two steps, we need to recalibrate our decisions and execution accordingly. If something changes materially in the latter two steps, we must ensure that we have adequate reasoning and analysis to justify it.

The Dynamic Mindset is about understanding and embracing the influence of time and change on problem solving and balancing these influences with relevant mechanisms so that the integrity of the problem-solving process is not impacted. It is about being flexible while remaining cohesive. This mindset is encapsulated by the question: *How can I maintain flexibility and cohesion in my problem-solving endeavour?*

"TIME IS A DRESSMAKER SPECIALIZING IN ALTERATIONS" – FAITH BALDWIN

Σ

The three mindsets presented above form the final component of the problem-solving methodology. In essence they distil to 3 things: being discerning, working with the end in mind, and being prepared for change. They are about mental astuteness and agility. MAP-MODEL-MINDSET. With the right mindset, the right process and the right understanding, we are very well set up to solve any problem that comes our way.

"YOU KNOW MY METHODS. APPLY THEM" –
SHERLOCK HOLMES

AFTERWORD

Our first sensation of a problem is when we feel the need to stop and think about something peculiar. For some problems, a solution can be devised and implemented quickly. For others, it takes longer. This book presented an intuitive yet powerful question-based approach for solving problems. By asking the right questions in the right sequence, we can unravel problems, opening the path to their resolution. Once we have understood this fundamental approach, we can use it to solve problems of all kinds and in all contexts.

> *"WHERE THERE IS A WILL, THERE IS A WAY" - PROVERB*

There is however something more to problem solving. This is the sense of personal conviction and optimism. Every problem can be solved. The main thing required is the will, the persistence and determination to solve it. At first, there must be a belief that a problem can be solved. This belief must be accompanied by a willingness to resolve the problem. Problem solving is about taking deliberate action. It is about making a conscious decision to engage the problem-solving process to find a solution. It is about choosing optimism over helplessness, engagement over apathy and courage over timidity.

The fable of the thirsty crow comes to mind. On a hot day, a thirsty crow flew far and wide in search for water, without luck. Finally, he saw a pitcher that contained some water. Alas, the water level was too low and the neck of the pitcher was too narrow for him to reach. The pitcher was too heavy for him to tilt. Instead of being disheartened and resigning himself to fate, the crow persisted. Then, he found some pebbles nearby and that gave him an idea. He began picking the pebbles and dropping them in the pitcher. Slowly, the water rose to a level he could drink from; and he quenched his thirst. Moral of the story: where there is a will, there is a way.

EVERY PROBLEM CAN BE SOLVED.

The mantra for successful problem-solving is starting optimistically, being systematic, and, persevering until the problem is solved.

The methodology presented in this book provides the reader with a toolset, skillset and mindset to solve problems. By doing so, it wishes to infuse the reader with the confidence to combat problems optimistically - and authoritatively.

REFERENCES

1. Ackoff, R. L. (1989). From Data to Wisdom. *Journal of Applied Systems Analysis, 16.*
2. *80/20 rule AKA: The Pareto principle webinar.* (2018, February 28). Juran. https://www.juran.com/resources/webinars/the-pareto-principle
3. *Design kit.* (2021). Design Kit. https://www.designkit.org/methods/3
4. Manning, A. (n.d.). Divergent vs. convergent thinking: How to strike a balance. *Harvard Division of Continuing Education Blogs.* https://blog.dce.harvard.edu/professional-development/divergent-vs-convergent-thinking-how-strike-balance
5. Eberle, B. (2008). Scamper: Creative games and activities for imagination development.
6. *Creating a culture of innovation - Google workspace. (n.d.).* Google Workspace (Formerly G Suite): Business Collaboration Tools. https://workspace.google.com/intl/en_nz/learn-more/creating_a_culture_of_innovation.html
7. Miller, G. A. (1956). The magical number seven, plus or minus two: Some limits on our capacity for processing information. *Psychological Review, 63*(2), 81-97. https://doi.org/10.1037/h0043158

8. *The feeling of throwing good money after bad: The role of affective reaction in the sunk-cost fallacy.* (2019, January 8).
   PLOS. https://journals.plos.org/plosone/article?id=10.1371/journal.pone.0209900
9. Robson, D. (2019, October 3). *The bias that can cause catastrophe.*
   BBCpage. https://www.bbc.com/worklife/article/20191001-the-bias-behind-the-worlds-greatest-catastrophes
10. *What we miss when we judge a decision by the outcome.* (2016, September 2). Harvard Business Review. https://hbr.org/2016/09/what-we-miss-when-we-judge-a-decision-by-the-outcome
11. (n.d.). IDEO | Design Thinking. https://designthinking.ideo.com
12. Stationery Office. (2017). *Managing successful projects with PRINCE2.* Stationery Office Books (TSO).
13. *Critical thinking.* (2020, October 15). Research & Learning Online. https://www.monash.edu/rlo/research-writing-assignments/critical-thinking
14. Cottrell, S. (2005). *Critical thinking skills.* Palgrave Macmillan.

*Images on p29 and p30 taken from openclipart.org {Public domain}

APPENDICES

1. PROBLEM SOLVING QUESTIONS

ACTIVITY	QUESTIONS
Discover the Problem	• What has come to our attention? • When does (or will) the problem occur? • Where is the problem happening? • What is the impact? • Who is impacted? • Why (and how) is the problem happening? • What is important?
Define the Goal	• What is our actionable goal statement?
Devise the Solution	• What are some ideas to pursue? • What are our criteria? • What is the best solution?
Deploy the Solution	• What is our action plan? • How to confirm success?

2. PROBLEM SOLVING WORKSHEET

ACTIVITY	METHOD	NOTES
Discover the Problem What is happening?	7W+H	
Define the Goal What is success?	H M W How Might We	
Devise the Solution What is our strategy?	Desirable-Feasible-Viable	
Deploy the Solution What is our action plan?	Activity Plan	

3. PROBLEM SOLVING CANVAS

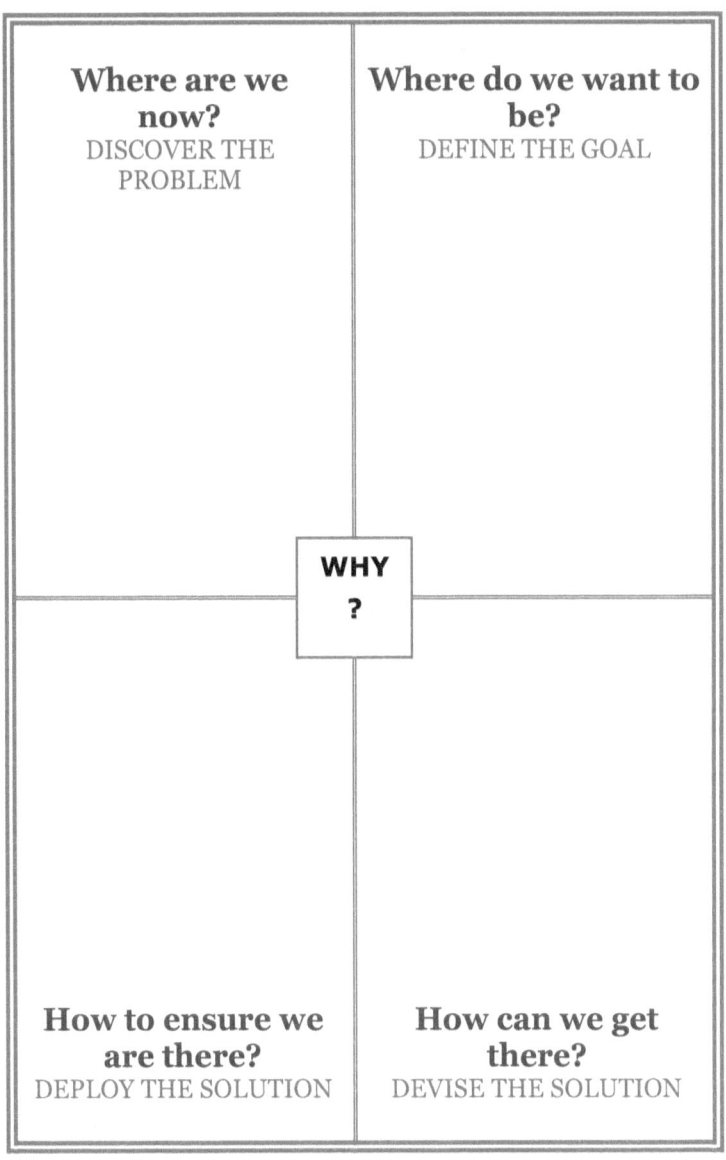

4. CASE STUDY

CAREER CRISIS

Hans is a middle-aged executive with 18 years' experience. Since losing his job 8 months ago, he's not been able to find new employment, despite his extensive experience and versatile skills.

What should he do?

Problem-solving is about discrepancy and effort. There is a discrepancy. Correcting it requires effort.

DISCOVER

Hans starts his problem-solving journey by using the Problem-Solving Canvas to take stock of his present situation: where am I now, and why am I here?

Using the 7W+H method, he first demarcates the key indicators: job loss, low job ads and scarce interview calls. Hans had been aware of this issue for some time; the job loss brought it into focus. The emergence of AI and the economic downturn indicate to Hans that this is not a fleeting event, but a signal of lasting change in his line of work, which will likely continue to shrink in the future. While the market is tight across the board, it's more acute in the mid-senior roles that he targets.

Although Hans is not the sole breadwinner, his career crisis inevitably impacts his family members. Hans acknowledges this, and thinks about who will be affected, and how. Quantifying the financial and emotional impact makes it evident to Hans that he must resolve this problem sooner rather than later.

The questions asked so far (what, when, where, who) give Hans a good foundation to delve into the deeper cause(s) of the problem. Why is the problem happening? How did things come to this?

Hans starts to think of plausible causes. He starts by focussing on his strengths. Feedback from recruiters has consistently affirmed his strong skill set. Skill obsolescence is not a cause. Discarding a non-issue is also part of causal analysis. His professional network, however, is not as robust or useful as it used to be, which does not help his cause.

In the aftermath of the post-pandemic downturn, companies are cutting jobs. This has created increased competition for mid-senior roles, which are also facing pressure from junior entrants. The industry is poised for disruption and likely to shrink. Hans' generalist skills, sought after in the past, are much less valuable now. The present market prefers specialists, a trend he feels will persist. Despite strong knowledge and versatile skills, Hans' lack of extended experience in one particular specialization is becoming a disadvantage. These, he feels, are the two most important underlying causes.

Hans has a good picture of his current situation, and the driving forces behind it. More than just a job crisis, external conditions and intrinsic factors have combined to put him in a complex *career crisis*, that has long term implications.

DEFINE

Having a gap relative to his career expectations. Using the insights from the Discovery phase, he starts to develop the actionable goal statement. Where do I want to be? He ponders. Given that this gap pertains to an open-ended and as yet undefined aspiration, rather than a fixed target, Hans will have considerable flexibility in defining the goal.

Using the HMW format, he creates an actionable goal statement that reflects his true problem, and guides him towards a realistic and effective solution.

It's normal to iterate though a HMW statement. A sample thought process is presented. For individual situations, HMW can read How Might I or HMI.

HMI find a job? Since it's framed as a question, its more conducive to ideation than an imperative like "I need to find a job". While finding a job is the end goal, discovery suggests that Hans needs to rejuvenate his career in the long term. He also does not want to preclude career development options or the possibility of working in a new industry.

A broader horizon is targeted: *HMI reinvent my career?* Although this captures his intent, it's vague (reinvent career – for what?) and does not capture the end goal (employment).

Hans iterates again and comes up with:

- *HMI become more employable?*

He feels this statement has sufficient focus and is broad enough to include both job search and career development strategies such as pursuing further education or transitioning to a different field.

Hans is aware that he does not have unlimited time and resources. His career crisis affects his household, which is an important consideration. He gives himself

1 year to achieve his goal, and a $10,000 budget. For the moment, he opts to omit these constraints from his HMI statement, to allow a wide exploration of solutions, but will factor them into his solution selection criteria.

DEVISE

The actionable goal statement provides Hans with sufficient direction and flexibility to pursue a wide variety of solution ideas.

Subject to this time and budget constraints, he comes up with 3 ideas, and uses the Desirable-Feasible-Viable method to evaluate them. Using DFV ensures that the idea(s) taken forward are robust across all three aspects, and have an inherent foundation for success. Finer criteria can be applied later to differentiate or prioritize further.

- Idea 1: *transition from generalist to specialist, and continue in the same industry.* The low change impact of this idea – industry and general skill area remains the same, makes it feasible and desirable. It's viability however is diminished due to Hans' lack of confidence in the long-term potential of his present industry.

- Idea 2: *do a course and transition to an upcoming growth industry.* The idea is feasible and desirable, but demands considerable time and investment. The upside of the idea however, Hans feels, would compensate for viability risks.
- *Idea 3: Entrepreneurship?* Why not try something radical!? He loves the idea. Initial research however suggests that it's not at all feasible for his situation, and has questionable viability also.

Idea 3 is discarded. Between ideas 1 and 2, Hans feels that overall, Idea 2 is closer to that sweet spot where Desirability-Feasibility-Viability intersect, than Idea 1.

Within Idea 2, let's say Hans is considering two study programmes. He now uses finer criteria (e.g., industry potential, ability to satisfy admission requirements etc), to pick the most suitable one.

Hans has found a solution that will help him meet his goal of becoming employable again. More importantly, the process of refining his goal statement and solution ideas has heightened his awareness of the rationale for his choices.

DEPLOY

With the solution chosen, Hans enters action mode. He makes a plan of action. There are multiple things to get in order – enrol in the course, find ways to finance the course, consult with household members on how to adapt to this major change etc.

Hans also needs to keep motivated when doing the course. For solutions that have a long implementation time, it is easy to lose focus and motivation. Hans however is confident in his choices and knows why he's chosen them. This will keep him in good stead.

In his actionable goal statement, Hans used the term employable. This can be measured by metrics such as interview calls, employment trends etc. Hans has a good basis for evaluating his success. ✓

ABOUT THE AUTHOR

Σ

PRATEEK VASISHT is an operational and organizational improvement consultant with experience across various industry sectors. He specializes in designing operating models, lean processes and continuous improvement frameworks. As a Lean advocate and business design enthusiast, he also blogs on these topics. An avid football fan, he is also the author of two football books: Football Masters, and The FIFA World Cup Finals Reimagined. He is passionate about environmental conservation and will donate 100% of the proceeds from this book to wildlife rehabilitation programmes. Prateek is based in Auckland, New Zealand.

Ω

www.ingramcontent.com/pod-product-compliance
Lightning Source LLC
Chambersburg PA
CBHW031427210526
45464CB00005B/2082